Mountain Top Musing III

Reflections

Reflections

Written By

Pete McKechnie

To Melanie and Melissa
Be kind, Wherever you can

[signature]

Design and Layout by

Nancy Smaroff

"On a lonely night, I reach out...
and find myself seeing the stars,
watching the shadows cast
by the full moon's dance.

I wonder,
what is beneath those shadows?
What lies in waiting?
And I sense,
it is connection hidden in the shadows."

~ Pete McKechnie

Forward

When we can see a piece of ourselves in everyone, and everything, we will have found the path to God.

Much of this book is inspired by relationship; with others, with life and with self. What we focus on is what will present, good or bad, because we cannot see anything that is not a reflection of our truths, even if they are not our Truth.

The poem "The Reflection" begins this book, and I find truth in it. What we are willing to witness will dictate our perception of the world.

The poem "Faith and Destiny" ends the book. Even when we lose a part of ourselves along the way, if it is true to our heart, it will come back. It is our path.

Angels have many faces.
So be open. Be aware.
When someone offers
A voice of gratitude,
Just accept it
And understand,
For just a moment,
You were the Angel.

Contents

The Reflection 1

Perspectives... 2

Gratitude Accepted.. 3

Listen 4

Honoring Self 5

Feeding the Heart 6

The Gem 7

The Dance... 8

By Virtue of Breaking 10

Crumbling Walls..11

Hello Again 12

Connection 13

Daring to Love 14

End-Full Beginnings 15

My Life Is Love 16

Live, Love, Laugh 17

Beauty of the Dance...18

Each Moment's Gifts...19

Experiencing True Connection 20

To Give and To Receive...21

Loving Self..22

Expression 23

Arrival..24

Into the Tempest 25

Do You Love?...26

New Year's Eve...28

In Service of What? 30

Resonance...31

Finding Myself...32

On Your Terms 34

Look 36

Being Seen 37

Speaking Through the Heart 38

Today 39

Being Authentic 40

Living Our Truth 42

The Road I Choose 43

One True Love 44

Gratitude 45

Inspiration 46

Subliminal Messages 47

Worth the Risk 48

Regret 49

One and the Same 50

The Many Faces of Angels 52

True Depth of Gratitude 53

Thank You 54

I Am 55

Happy Thanks Giving 56

Outside, Looking In 57

Climbing to My Truth 58

Path of the Heart 60

The Lamp 61

Shifting Sands 62

Just Myself 63

Faith and Destiny 64

—
x

The Reflection

Life is lived
In the reflection.
Meaning is found
In what draws us,
Or repels.

Life is lived
In the reflection.
We meet everything
From where we stand.
What we are willing
To witness
In this mirrored world
Will define the depths
At which we allow
Our spirits to dance.

Life is
The Reflection.

Perspectives

You don't have to
Agree with me.
You don't have to
See things my way.
And I don't have to
Agree with you or
See things your way.

But I will, ultimately, have to
Understand that your perspective
Is as authentic as mine,
And, ultimately,
You will have to
Accept the same.

So, while I do not have to
Agree with you,
And you do not have to
Agree with me,
We will both have to
Understand that the majesty
Of this world
Is big enough
For more than one perspective.

Gratitude Accepted

It can be challenging enough
In this life
To feel gratitude.
To look beyond the mundane
And allow oneself to be
Fully grateful for each moment.

This challenge pales, however,
With the full understanding of gratitude.
It pales to the possibility
Of looking into another spirit's eyes,
And hearing a voice
Express the gratitude they feel
For you.

It pales when those words are welcomed,
Without ego or agenda,
And we accept the gratitude of others,
Simply acknowledging and honoring
Someone else's gratitude for us.

When we can do both,
Live with gratitude for all
And understand that life
Is grateful for us,
Our hearts will have learned
To open.

Listen

I can hear your words,
But if I will not listen,
They will fall on deaf ears.
You can hear mine,
But if you choose to do the same,
My words as well
Will fail to resonate.

So, let us agree,
Let us come together and decide,
That if I choose to utter a word,
I will do so only with the promise
That I will listen to yours.
And when you speak,
You will do the same,
And agree to listen to mine.

Honoring Self

Who among us
Does not yearn to matter?
Who among us
Would not love to know
That those around us
Honored us,
Valued us?

I can think of no one.

Who among us
Fully understands
That until they matter
To themselves,
And honor their own gifts,
Valuing the presence
Only they can reflect,
They will not achieve
The goal of mattering,
Being honored?

Who among us
Understands that the path
To being honored by others
Begins with our own ability
To honor ourselves?

Feeding the Heart

It is not what I need of you
That matters,
Nor is it what you need of me.
It will not matter
In the long run
If you need from me,
And the notion that I need from you
Will fade as well.

What matters is
What you need of yourself,
And what matters to me
Is the same.

What matters
Is that you feed your heart
While I am feeding my own.
And should we play a part
In the truth of each other's hearts,
Our hearts will have the chance
To revel in the dance.

The Gem

Each connection we make
Holds a promise, a gem.
Each soul we meet
Is a beacon.

It may seem
From the start
That the meeting
Is worthless,
Or it may seem
From the beginning
That a diamond
Has been found.
Either way
Each connection we make
Holds a promise.

When we understand,
We will see,
That the diamond and the stone
Offer the same gift
And if we allow it,
Both, ultimately,
Will bring us
To the understanding
That we are the Gem.

The Dance

Lonely,
And from across
The room
I see you.
I feel the pull
Of connection,
Of destiny.
Toward you I walk.
"Might I have this dance,"
I ask?

Holding out my hand
You take mine in yours,
And we dance...

We dance
Like the wind
Through the leaves.
We dance
Like the waves
On the shore.
We dance, together,
As we have
Never danced before.

As the dance ends,
I find myself… alone.

From across the room
I see you.
I understand the pull
Of connection,
Of destiny.
Toward you I walk.
"Thank you for the dance,"
I say.

I reach out my hand.
You take mine in yours,
And say,
"Yes, Thank You."

By Virtue of Breaking

By virtue of breaking,
A heart learns to live.
And by learning to live
A heart comes to understand
Its Truth, its Destiny.

By virtue of breaking,
A heart learns to give.
And by learning to give,
A heart comes to understand
Its Fullness, its Destiny.

While this path
Might seem cruel, unnecessary,
It is true that in breaking,
A heart learns to be whole.
And in becoming whole
The Heart will understand
Authentic love.
And by virtue of breaking,
The Heart will learn to heal.

Crumbling Walls

I know that I hide.
I know that I keep close council,
My heart protected
Behind strong walls.
I also know
That this protection
Is an illusion,
And that any chance given
To offer my heart
I will take.

What I have come to see
Is that the best protection,
I have to offer my heart,
Lies within the willingness
To offer it completely.
Should I not take this risk,
And give my heart completely,
I will not be able
To offer my heart at all.

For there is a part of me
That knows,
When I do not find a way
To offer my heart,
There is nothing left
For me to give.

Hello Again

What is this I feel
Stirring my soul
With recollections of lives past,
Manifesting before my eyes,
Recognized instantly in my spirit
And remembered fully in my heart?

Could it be?
Can I trust this intuition
That draws me forth?
It pulls me ever nearer,
Guiding me gently
Toward recognition.

Is it possible?
Is that you?

I wonder...
Back from times long gone,
Forgotten in this man's mind,
Yet, remembered completely in my soul,
Come back to take your place
By my side
As my dearest friend.

Connection

It is the nature of the world
That we should reach out
And take a chance.
The world will return
This action
With connection.
It might not be a connection
We can understand
Or one that was expected,
But, none-the-less,
Connection will occur.

Daring to Love

Should I love
Without knowing
What will be given back?

Should I love
Without the knowing
That my love
Will fall into an open heart?

Yes, I should love,
And if not returned
Or welcomed into an open heart,
At least I will know
That I Loved.

End-Full Beginnings

A beginning has no chance,
Has no ability
To become incipient,
Without the understanding
That it will ultimately be born
In the wake of an ending.

They are tied, inevitably,
To one another,
As neither one can exist
Without the other.

So, I find it strange
That endings bring with them
Such un-surety,
Even though without them,
The excitement and rejuvenation
Of the next beginning
Would remain unfelt
And out of reach.

As much as I might
Enjoy the thrill of beginnings,
Let me live, also,
To brave the waters of endings
With joy, and knowledge,
That endings are nothing more
Than the passage of birth
To the new.

My Life Is Love

The life I have built
Are the things I have around me.
The trials and tribulations,
Joys and sorrows,
I find myself in
At the moment.
If I find myself too attached
To these things,
What might I give up
To maintain them?

The love I have built
Is the peace I find within me,
The connections made
Through joys and sorrows
That I find myself in
At the moment.
If I find myself too attached
To these things,
I would let go of all
To keep them.

My life is circumstance,
A hand dealt,
And should I choose
To value it above all else,
I would have sold my soul.
My love is who I am,
And if I choose to value it,
My life will become a script
Within which my soul will sing.

Live, Love, Laugh

I can live,
I can love,
I can laugh.
But until I reach the place
Where I understand
That my life,
My love,
My laughter,
Is no more important
Than the life I give others,
The love I inspire
Or the laughter I give,
I will not fully
Have lived,
Loved
Or laughed.

Let me understand
That if I give life,
Give love,
And offer the opportunity
For others to laugh,
I will have
Lived,
Loved
And laughed,
And that will,
In the end,
Suffice.

Beauty of the Dance

Would you notice the color
Of the face of the man
If his heart's worn in a smile?
Would you notice the color
Of the skin of the hand?
Sit back and think a while.

Would you notice the color
Of the face of the man
If you could see into his soul?
Would you notice the color
Of the skin of the hand
If it lifts you and helps you to grow?

When two hearts come together,
And two souls take the chance,
When two can face the world
And ignore the ignorance,
Would you notice the color
Of the face of the man
Or see the beauty of the dance?

Each Moment's Gifts

I do not find myself
Happy
In every moment I experience.
I am not always fed
As I sit in silence, alone.

But I understand
That if I cannot
Be with the gifts
Each moment brings.
If I choose not
To be present
When I am feeling unfulfilled,
My chance to be present
When I have the opportunity
To feel most whole
Will be lost as well.

So I will be present.
I will be here now,
When I am feeling most lost,
Because if I am not,
I will not be able
To be present
When the chance comes along
For me to be found.

Experiencing True Connection

Is there, truly, a difference
Between the connection
With those I will never meet
And the connection
With those I hold most dear?

Or is it simply true
That what I will
Allow myself to express,
With those held
Closest to my heart,
Will dictate the way I experience
My connection to this world?

To Give and To Receive

If you should give a gift,
Give it unrequited
Give it without thought.
Simply open
And offer.

When you do this,
You will find
That in allowing,
You will allow the gift
To be given back.

So give,
Simply give.
But understand
That should you deny
Another's attempt
To give to you,
You will deny
Your own ability
To receive the gift.

Loving Self

Life is the process
Of coming
To love oneself.

It is the grandest affair
In which,
Hopefully,
Our fears and insecurities,
Our self-loathing and distrust
Are overcome.

Ultimately,
When acceptance prevails,
We simply say
To ourselves,

I Do!

Expression

Expression
Is a gift we all desire,
A wish to be heard
All of us
Can understand.
But in truth,
It is completely
"Miss"understood.

Expression
Is not about being heard.
It is not about having a voice.
Expression is not
About thought,
Or words,
Or even intentions.
Expression is being,
Simply being.

In truth, it is not
Expression
We all desire.
It is simply that
What we Express
In this life
Will be seen.

Arrival

I will have arrived
When I find
That no one's words
Will sway my heart
Or impact my soul.

I will have arrived
When I understand
That the words of others
Are not a reflection of me
And do not carry weight.

It is only how
I interpret
And allow those words
To direct my path
That has weight.

That is on me,
The listener,
Not on the speaker
Of the words.

I will have arrived
When I find
That my truth
Can never be spoken
Through the words of others,
My truth will be made clear
Through my response.

Into the Tempest

When the thunder crashes,
And the wind
Rips leaves from the trees,
It is easy to see
That the tempest has come.

The storm has arrived,
And though it is our choice
To dance in the wind
Or cower in the corner,
It is not clear
That our choices
Have brought this storm to pass.

All storms
Are preceded by stillness,
And thunder cannot crash
Without the dance
Of opposing forces.
It is a choice
To engage and connect,
With each other,
Which not only creates the tempest,
But, also, gives us the chance,
The Grace,
To dance in the rain.

Do You Love?

Life is a lesson,
And it asks a simple question.
Do you love me?
Do you love?

Most will spend
Much of their time
Defining love
Around agenda.
They will decide
For themselves
What is worthy of love,
And they will have
Missed the point.

Can we be
Born in the image of God
And not understand that reality?

Many will miss the point, again,
And define for themselves
An image of God,
And love only what
They believe
Their God will love.

Most will not understand
That their God loves all,
And the only question
God cares about is,
Do you Love?

New Year's Eve

There is no doubt
In my mind
That at some point
In the past,
On the Eve
Of a New Year,
Someone, somewhere,
Was feeling what I feel now.
And there is no doubt
In my mind
That at some point
In the future,
On the Eve
Of a New Year,
Someone, somewhere,
Will be feeling what I feel now.

There is, also, no doubt
In my mind
That those from the past
Could not have imagined
My circumstance,
And that I cannot imagine
The circumstance
Of a future soul.

Times change too fast,
And the challenges
We all face
Change along with the times.

There is no doubt,
In my mind,
That on the Eve
Of a New Year,
We all, throughout time,
Hope for peace, and love, and joy
As one year
Gives way
To possibilities
Of the New.

So, regardless of circumstance,
Without respect
To what has been
Or will be,
Peace, Love, and Joy
To us all
As we enter,
What truly is,
Just another year.

In Service of What?

Any thought I may have
That serves me,
I should question.
Anytime my thoughts
Push me in a direction
That I wish to go
I should pause
And wonder.
Not who I am serving, but what?

If the answer
Is that I am
Choosing to serve myself,
At the expense
Of all else
That makes
This Universe sing,
I hope to find the grace
To make a better choice.

To understand
The note I play
In this symphony
Is merely a tiny portion
Of the song.

Resonance

Resonance is not a choice,
It is a truth.
It cannot be chosen
Or directed,
And is neither
Optional
Nor deniable,
It simply is.

When resonance
Presents itself,
We will choose,
To accept the truth
Or we will deny
That which is most true
Of ourselves.

Finding Myself

I miss you.
Easy words to speak,
But they hide
A greater truth.

It is not
You I miss.
As much as I miss
The feeling
Of holding you
In my arms.

As much as I miss
Your presence,
I find I miss more
The person I was,
In your arms,
And in your presence.

I find I miss more
The person you showed me
I could be.

While I miss you,
It is not you so much
That I miss,
Rather that I miss
The notion of
Finding myself
That you so clearly
Gifted to me.

So, I thank you for this.
Because in missing you
I just might manage
To find myself.

On Your Terms

It can be painful
To live life
On your own terms.
You may risk
The disappointed
Expressions,
The judgmental words
Of those closest to you.

When you make
The choice
To live life
On your own terms,
You may well
Feel alone,
Alienated.

But what happens
When you live a life
On the terms of others?

Ultimately,
You will disappoint yourself.
You will become
Alienated from your truth.
You will be left alone in a crowd
Where your light cannot shine.

So, while it can be painful
To let your own light shine,
It is far more painful to dull it
Within the numbness
Of acceptance.

Look

Look closely, look deeply, understand the gift of my life.

It is not what I do. It is not my trials or my habits.
It is not my daily tribulations or the turmoil in which
I so often find myself.

If it were these things, I could offer you no peace, and
my gift to you would be of no more value than your
gift to me would be if it were the same.

Look closely, look deeply, and see. My gift to you is my
heart, and like all hearts mine has flaws, and longs only
for understanding.

With this understanding, open your heart to mine, and
allow our hearts simply to

Dance.

Being Seen

I believe that
I will never be seen
When my daily purpose
Is to be so.
I will not
Be understood or heard,
When my actions are
Geared toward this result.

Wanting to
Be seen, understood and heard,
Will undermine my efforts.

If I wish to be seen,
I will simply have to
Present myself.
If I wish to be understood,
I will have to
Be authentic.
If I wish to be heard,
I will simply have to
Speak my truth, and
I will have to do this,
Regardless of how
It is perceived.

Speaking Through the Heart

Communication is
A misunderstood art.
We think it depends
On words,
On eloquence
And even on argument.
It does not.

Words, eloquence,
And argument,
Are more likely to
Negate communication
Than to foster it.

Perhaps we should learn
To close our mouths,
Open our hearts
And understand
That our minds
Will never choose
The words that
Our hearts so clearly
Wish to speak,
And our minds
Will never hear
With the clarity
We achieve
When we listen
With the Heart.

Today

"There will come a day,"
Perhaps the most dangerous
Thought we can have.

There will come a day to... to what?
To live?
To express?
To love?

The day will never come
To do those things
Until we understand
That the only day to do them
Is Today.

Being Authentic

I will tell you the truth.
In doing so
I will gift you.
I will show you
Who I am,
Where I am,
What I am,
And in doing so
Give you the choice
To accept me
Or not.

I ask the same of you.
I ask that you
Not paint
A pretty picture.
I ask that you not
Present to me what
You would like
For me to see.

I ask simply the for truth.
I ask simply
For what I am willing
To give you.
I ask simply
That you show me
Who you are,
Where you are,
What you are,
And that you gift me
With the choice
I am willing to grant you,
The gift of Authenticity.

Living Our Truth

We are
Who we show the world,
And through the grace of love,
We will show the world
The nature of our heart.

If we do not,
We will forever be judged
And held back by the illusion
That we present as ourselves.

The Road I Choose

I am going where I am going,
Regardless.
The destination is irrelevant.
I can, however,
Sit in traffic and bitch
Or sit in traffic
And use that time
To witness life,
To take in
Everything that presents.

I am going where I am going,
Regardless.
Will I enjoy this ride?
Well, darling,
That is totally
Up to me.
I can bitch
Or take in.
I can look at the taillights
Or use the time
To see life's dance
In the median.

I am going where I am going.
It is my choice
To go there
Willingly,
Happily,
Knowingly
Or not.

One True Love

True love should destroy us.
True love should devastate.
True love should bring us to our knees.
Why?

Only when we are destroyed,
Devastated, and brought to our knees
Will we understand.
In order for us to fully receive,
We will have to fully give.
And to give, fully,
We will have to understand
That we will never receive
A love greater
Than we are willing to offer.

Gratitude

G racefully awaiting,
  R eceptive, open to life.
    A lways ready
      T o chance a mystery.
        I walk this path,
          T oday's gifts
            U nfolding,
              D esiring little other than
                E xperience.

Inspiration

Inspiration leads to fruition.
That is not to say
It will be easy
Or require no effort,
And it is not to say
It will come quickly.

Inspiration
Is the voice of something
Far grander than we are.
When we listen to it,
It has no option
Other than to actualize.

Subliminal Messages

We are taught to kill
The enemy, perhaps,
Or fear.
We are taught to overcome,
Prevail, win.
We are taught that life
Is a perpetual struggle,
And that there is no path
Out of this life
Other than to fight.

What would happen
If we were simply
Taught to love?
What would we lose,
Other than the notion
That everyone else
Is out to destroy us?

What if we just chose
Loving over killing?
Tell me,
Would this really
Make our lives
Less fulfilling?

Worth the Risk

All connection involves risk.
We can't connect
Without opening,
And we cannot open
Without the possibility
That we will be shut down.

What would happen, though,
If we do not open,
And accept the risk
Of connection?
We would be safe,
And no one would shut us down,
But only because we chose,
On our own,
To close the doorway
To our Heart.

Regret

Yes, I regret.
I regret things said,
Or left unsaid.
I regret actions taken
And those I failed to take
For fear of regret.
I regret connections,
Both connections made
That ended in fire
And connections not made
Whose potential
Will never actualize.

Yes, I regret.
I regret missed-targets
And targets my aim
Were never meant to pierce.
Mostly, however, I regret
That I never understood
That regret is the key
That will ultimately
Open the door
To my destiny.

So, I welcome my past regrets,
As I will welcome
The ones yet to come,
Because I know
If I don't take chances
I might regret,
I might miss taking the one
That will set me free.

One and the Same

"I don't know you."
These are powerful words,
And have led
To most of the world's
Destruction.
What we don't know
We willingly destroy;
If I don't know you,
My choice is easy.

"I do know you."
Powerful words as well,
And perhaps will lead
The world to salvation.
Because even if we have not met,
I might understand,
That you want nothing more
Than I do.
You want life, as do I
And we do not need
To know each other
To understand that desire.

I don't know you,
But I know YOU,
And you know nothing
Of me,
But you know all that
Is important to ME.

When we choose to understand this,
We will understand,
That your life
And mine
Are one and the same,
And we will both
Live or die
In this truth.

The Many Faces of Angels

It was cold.
The early spring-breeze
Filtering through the fabric of my shirt,
Chilling my flesh.
I sat hand-in-hand
With the woman I loved,
Lamenting the difficulties of life
And the struggles that lie ahead.
Wondering why the chosen path
Should be so full of pain.

An old man approached,
Full, white beard and uncombed hair,
Clothes, held together with grime,
Hanging loosely on his battered frame.
Pushing his whole world, his identity,
In a single shopping cart.
With a twinkle in his eye, he passed,
And said simply,
"Isn't it a beautiful night?"

As my soul was cleansed
I pondered the riches of my life,
And turned to face the woman I loved.
Yes, indeed, I thought,
It is a beautiful night.

True Depth of Gratitude

True gratitude is overwhelming.
It rips the heart open,
And creates a space
Where only love can live.

True gratitude brings tears.
It fills one to the point
Where there is no option
But to overflow,
To explode in wonder
At what life
Might bring your way.

True gratitude is the greatest gift.
One only allowed to those
Willing to dive into
The depths of its ocean.

Thank You

I wish to express gratitude.
I wish to express this
From the deepest places
I will allow my heart to dive.

I am not sure
How to do this.
I am not sure
How to express
My level of gratitude
Without acknowledging
My weaknesses, my needs.

But this is what I wish to do,
And in this moment of weakness,
I have found the strength
To say thank you,
And feel for myself,
The truth of gratitude.

I Am

I am what I show
The world.

I am as much,
And only as much,
As I am willing
To expose.
Knowing this
And understanding
That my own comfort
In my binding skin,
Is the key
To my expression.

What should I do?
Strip down, I think,
Un-adorn myself,
Strip, I think,
And expose everything
That is real
Of me.

If I do not,
I will never show my truth
To the world.

Happy Thanks Giving

Happiness with circumstance is a wonderful feeling.
It is also often
Preceded or followed
By unhappiness with circumstance.

Happiness with circumstance is dependent.
Happiness with circumstance is contingent.
Dependent and contingent
On something outside
Of ourselves.

Thankfulness, on the other hand,
Knows nothing of circumstance,
And is neither preceded nor followed by anything
Other than moments where
Our heart chooses to close the door.

Thankfulness, neither dependent or contingent
On circumstance,
Is simply the expression of an open heart.
A willingness to see
The beauty of all
Through circumstance
And to understand that life,
In its entirety,
Is God's Gift to us.

Thankfulness is the Gift offered;
The Gift of an open heart.

Outside, Looking In

So much of my life
I have spent
Feeling a disconnect.
Being outside, looking in,
As if my life
Would be so much better
If only I could walk
Through the door.

It has taken a while,
Years in fact,
To realize
I have actually been
Inside, looking out.
That I was
A part of everything,
Everything, except
What waited for me
Beyond the door.

Now I know,
That the path
To connection
Is to be outside,
Looking out.

Climbing to My Truth

The mountain before me
And the cliff
Seem insurmountable.
The climb, it seems,
Would lead to nothing
But a fall,
A fall to certain death.

But climb I do,
Hand over hand,
Clinging tightly
To the rocks, the cliffs.
The fear of falling
Only slightly less powerful
Than my desire to move,
To climb,
And to find
The truth over the horizon
Of the cliff.

My fingers bloodied,
Every muscle in my body aching,
I finally reach the summit
And pull myself over the ledge.

I rest for a moment
Before I look behind
And witness my climb.
Behind me I see
A hillside,
A pasture woven
With the trails of many.

An easy walk, really,
Through the tall grasses,
And now I understand.
There was never a cliff,
There was only a path,
A path that seemed
Insurmountable, impossible.

In fact, it was nothing more
Than a walk
Through the countryside,
Toward the place
That I recognize as My Truth.

Path of the Heart

Separate paths, kindred souls
Open a connection
Without proximity,
A Knowing
Without knowing.

The path of the heart
Will find this.
The path of the heart
Will understand this
And feel the connection.
The paths might be
Miles apart,
No hand-in-hand passage
Allowed.

The path of the heart
Won't care.
The path of the heart
Will just walk,
One step at time
To its destiny.
With this,
It will recognize
All hearts
Who walk the path
Of their own heart.

The Lamp

My hand gropes along the wall,
Cold plaster under my fingertips,
The room black,
Mirroring the darkness in my soul.

Searching for the switch which must be there,
Promising light and security,
Collisions with un-foreseen obstacles,
The walls of the room drawing in upon me,
Condenses darkness into fear.

My nervous hand quivers, then shakes,
Then trembles.
The switch seems elusive,
Just out of reach,
And the light that would guide me
Remains hidden or fails to shine
In my time of greatest need.

My heart beats wildly now
And the sweat pours,
My hand no longer able
To keep contact with the wall.
Unable to continue my outward search,
I stop and pull my hands to my chest,
Breathing deeply, slowly,
Until I reach a point of stillness.

As I slowly open my eyes,
The light floods in
And I remember,
It is my faith that is the Lamp.

Shifting Sands

I thought today to visit my past,
To travel to a distant shore
And revisit a time long ago.

As I considered this,
I began to understand.
If I make my trek,
The sand on which I would stand
Is not the same sand
I stood on as a child
And the waves
Which crashed on the shore
Would be no more familiar.

I began to understand
That I can only visit
A place I once knew
As it has become.
I can only visit it
In the form
As the person I have become.

As I ponder this,
I realize that while it is my past
Which has created
Who I am today,
It is, also, I who took part
In creating the present form
Of everyone in my past.

Just Myself

I'm just...

Just what... I wonder
A dad?
A guy?
A wannabe redneck
With liberal-leanings?

I'm just...

Just what?
I feel
The judgment
In the words
And wonder.

Is it just myself
I long to be?

Faith and Destiny

The old man awoke, a soft voice tickling the back of his mind. A voice he thought lost to him, an intuition dispersed when he left the farm and entered the city years ago.

Decimated by the Promised Land of urban life, he could barely hear the voice. Didn't hear it, really, but it guided him from his cardboard home underneath an overpass and into the city streets. Into the line of vision of the masses who avoided his presence, and sent psychic arrows into his already deadened heart. Their disgust clear for the 'homeless old man' he had become.

He walked, familiar with the stares, the fear, almost aimlessly until he saw a storefront. As he approached, two shoppers in front of the window saw him, scampered away in fear of a homeless old man and he took their place at the window.

> Drawn at once to the headless,
> velvet neck of a mannequin,
> he gazed in awe at a small silver locket,
> gracefully draped, elegant in its simplicity.
> Smooth and delicate as a flower,
> It grabbed him and held him.

> *The shop owner needs you to leave now.*
> A voice from nowhere said.

The old man turned to look
into the deepest eyes he had ever seen,
into the radiance of a beautiful young woman,
into a smile that carried the compassion
of a God he thought lost long ago.
He could do nothing but turn and walk away.

He was drawn back to the storefront over and over as
time went by, and each time it was the same. He would
approach the window as shoppers looked on and they
would leave in disgust, repelled by his presence.

He would stand,
gripped by the locket,
until the young woman would appear,
speaking gently and kindly —

The shop owner needs you to leave now.
She would smile and nod, and he would leave.

Until at last, he was drawn to the store and the locket
was gone. Taken from him, as he knew it must be
someday. Still, his heart collapsed, sank into the
depths of despair. As he turned to walk away...

He found himself, face to face,
with the young woman,
and she thought to him,
for he had realized she never moved her lips —

It is still there for you.

He understood, in a flood of intuition,
in an ocean of connection,
that he had held space.
He had made it possible
for the one who needed it most
to find the locket.
His intuition, his connection,
rushing back,
filling his heart and soul.

The young woman took his arm.
Walk with me, she thought.

And they walked.
With every step, the city changed,
becoming emerald green,
buildings waving in the air like fields of wheat.
The city morphed,
changing into the farmstead
he had called home as a child,
and his Guardian walked with him
as his childhood home came into view.

You have done what you were meant to do, she thought.

She held out her gentle hand.
As she opened it for him, he saw the locket.
As his hand reached out to accept the gift,
his wrinkles faded, his flesh firmed,
and it was a young man's hand that took the locket,
a young man's hands that opened the heart,
and a young man's eyes that read the single word
engraved inside the simple, silver heart.

As he broke into a run toward the old homestead,
his mother appearing on the porch
to welcome him home,
he read that word over and over in his mind.
In the end, he had finally regained his

FAITH

Ayana and Yoga

It is not our dissonance that separates us.
It is our unwillingness to experience our resonance.

Connections create
Pathways, one to another
Woven between hearts

Made in the USA
Lexington, KY
03 September 2018